HIDDEN TREASURES

WEST MIDLANDS

Edited by Allison Dowse

First published in Great Britain in 2003 by
YOUNG WRITERS
Remus House,
Coltsfoot Drive,
Peterborough, PE2 9JX
Telephone (01733) 890066

HB ISBN 0 75434 147 X
SB ISBN 0 75434 148 8

FOREWORD

This year, the Young Writers' Hidden Treasures competition proudly presents a showcase of the best poetic talent from over 72,000 up-and-coming writers nationwide.

Young Writers was established in 1991 and we are still successful, even in today's technologically-led world, in promoting and encouraging the reading and writing of poetry.

The thought, effort, imagination and hard work put into each poem impressed us all, and once again, the task of selecting poems was a difficult one, but nevertheless, an enjoyable experience.

We hope you are as pleased as we are with the final selection and that you and your family continue to be entertained with *Hidden Treasures West Midlands* for many years to come.

CONTENTS

St Paul's CE Primary School, Wolverhampton

Tividale Hall Primary School

Jack Fisher	106
Anthony Shipley	107
Manpreet Dhillon	108
Rhea Asfaw	109
Ryan Howells	110
Jack Moore	111
Michelle Humphrey	112
Emily Gates	113
Joe Lockley	114

Woodfield Junior School

Amrita Bisla	115
Rohini Devi	116
Cadi Evans	117
Lily Gelder	118
Zoe Hunter-Grewal	119
Rosie Inman	120
Dan Jones	121
Nidhi Mehan	122
Claire Nellany	123
Daniel Owen	124
Luke Price	125
Naveed Raza	126
James Robbins	127
Jennifer Robbins	128
Maninder Saggu	129
Sodhi Sahota	130
Adam Tustin	131
Alec White	132
Jonathan Woodall	133

Wyken Croft Primary School

Charlotte Kertrestel	134
Darren Haley	135
Leah Thompson	136
Hope Roberts-Dalton	137
David Sanders	138

The Poems

HIDDEN TREASURES

I dive into the water, what can I see?
A lovely jellyfish looking at me.
Then comes a dolphin he's so sublime,
Will he be here until the end of time?
My day is done but there is still a world
Out there under the sea.

Laura Harding (10)
Hasbury CE Primary School

HIDDEN TREASURES

As I close my curtains,
A silver slither falls into my room.
As I pass into my slumber,
I think of the moon,
As round as a coin,
As silver as the stars.
Sometimes these thoughts pass into dreams.
Will the moon last forever?

Stephanie Povey (10)
Hasbury CE Primary School

THE TREASURY

I was being a pain and it happened again
Teacher had a go at me
I had a go back
She told me to go out the class
And that was the end of that

I was running around and joking about
And it happened again
Teacher had a go at me
I had a go back
She sent me out the class
And that was the end of that

At home time I was staying after school
She had a go at me
And found out I made something
For her treasury.

Ruth Holloway (11)
Hasbury CE Primary School

DOLPHINS

Dolphins here,
Dolphins there,
Dolphins swimming everywhere.

They glide and swim and jump around,
Then they return home safe and sound.

Are we aware of the treasures of this creature?

Sadly the dolphin is not what it seems,
They get caught up in fish nets, rods and reams.

Are we aware of the treasures of this creature?

Dolphins here,
Dolphins there,
Dolphins swimming everywhere.

But for how long?

Katie James (11)
Hasbury CE Primary School

I'M AS SICK AS A GOAT!

I'm as sick as a goat,
I've lost mi flippin' boat,
I haven't got anything to row with,
Or to row in.

I'm as sick as a goat,
I've lost mi dam' boat,
I've had a bad day today,
So just leave me alone, OK.

Ryan McCauley (9)
Hasbury CE Primary School

FOOTBALL IS THE BEST

Football is the best,
Football in the net,
Balls flying around you,
Players running around you,
Goal! Goal! Goal!
It's the best, best, best!

Mark Malanaphy & Luke Phillips (7)
Our Lady And St Kenelm RC School

PROFESSOR PICKLEDEY PUDDLE

Professor Pickledey Puddle was always in a muddle,
Her ideas were atrocious, her potions absurd,
If she said anything, she was not heard.
Nobody trusted her, no one at all,
The people thought her brain was a brick wall!
She tried experiments (which were all a disaster),
She was often (at the end) covered in plaster!

I don't quite know why she decided to be a professor,
She finally realised and agreed on being
A disastrous *hairdresser!*

Esther Olive (7)
Our Lady And St Kenelm RC School

SEPTEMBER 11TH 2001

Planes crashing, lights flashing
Buildings burning, fire turning
People filing, men and women piling
Mums crying, people dying
Men thumping, women jumping
Towers crumbling, country rumbling
September 11th 2001.

Stephen Kirk (9) & Mark Carey (10)
Our Lady And St Kenelm RC School

THE HURRICANE

Hurricane coming,
Forecast warning.
Twisting and twirling,
Bashing and crashing,
Taking, breaking and shaking,
Cluttering and shuttering,
Smashing and clashing,
Screaming, running and hiding,
Shivering and shouting,
Crying and whining,
The whole town destroying!

Joanna Grennan (9)
Our Lady And St Kenelm RC School

THE BALLERINA

I put on my tutu and warm up,
Flowing like a dolphin in water,
The wonders of the stage, pointing, bending, stretching,
The best that I can do -
Leaping over imaginary walls, lengthening
And stooping, pausing on my toes, running softly,
Over delicate floorboards my shoes glide.
Look a troupe of dancers tiptoeing towards me,
Dainty movements -
I am better than they are! . . . The audience like me,
Flying silently across the stage.
Meekly hopping and skipping, them all clapping.
Is that my favourite ballet dancer,
Wearing a tiara, sweeping silently towards me?
My breath has vanished, too soon the show has finished.
Back in the changing rooms I meet her,
My dreams have come true.

Ailsa Suleman (9)
Our Lady And St Kenelm RC School

THE BUILDING SITE

The building site what a place,

Bricks smashing, bulldozers crashing,
Rain showering, animals cowering,
Builder's bum showing, women knowing,
Men tripping, trousers ripping,
Crane lifting, dust drifting,
Children sneezing, wind breezing,
Buildings falling, people calling,

The building site - things happening.

Michael Rodgers (10) & George Hammond (9)
Our Lady And St Kenelm RC School

ROBOT WARS EXTREME

Why watch Robot Wars Extreme?
Because . . .

Robots are flipping and gripping,
Moving and grooving,
Pinning and spinning,
Bashing, crashing and lashing,
Turning and burning,
Oiling and spoiling,
Splitting and hitting.

The crowds are screaming and dreaming,
Hearing and cheering,
Bumping and thumping,
The destroying is annoying,
Roaring, falling and hauling,
Tipping and snipping,
Holding and folding,
Swearing and sharing
And then we all hear, 'Seize!'

John O'Toole (9)
Our Lady And St Kenelm RC School

ROBOT WARS EXTREME

Why watch Robot Wars Extreme?
Because . . .
Robots are flipping, grabbing and bashing
Sawing and spinning
Crashing and flaming
Pinning and winning
Spilling and oiling
Singing and banging
Turning and making
Falling and cheering
Destroying and crashing
Roaring and refereeing
And then we hear, 'Seize!'

Joshua Alcock (10)
Our Lady And St Kenelm RC School

FIREWORKS!

Fireworks are:
    Crashing and bashing,
    Thumping and bumping,
    Flashing and lashing.

Crowds are:
    Clapping, tapping and gazing,
    Saying, 'That's amazing!'
    Here comes the grand finale.

Children are:
    Shouting and screaming
    And waving and laughing.

Fireworks are:
    Booming,
    It's a great display.
    Oh no, it's all over,
    Time to go.

Margaret O'Toole (9)
Our Lady And St Kenelm RC School

THE WORLD CUP

Fans arriving, it's very exciting,
Players are warming up,
Cheering and clapping,
Booing and hissing.

It's kick-off, shouting and singing,
While players are playing,
Shooting and booting. 'Oh, what a great goal!'
Celebrating and singing - it's very exciting!

Fowling and howling,
Kicking and hitting,
Running and passing,
Oh, what a miss!

The final whistle blowing,
Picking up the cup,
Crowd erupting,
Crowd roaring.

Sean Kilgallon & Matthew Reilly (9)
Our Lady And St Kenelm RC School

SPACEMAN

I put on my helmet and get in my rocket
Blasting off as I look for stars
The secrets of the universe.
Along my way, on and on I look -
Over the moon, when I look, stars.
Then as I look, asteroids - bang, bang, bang!
Look, Pluto, all holes in it.
Does that hole on Pluto have aliens in?
Is that the planet Mars?
Wow!

I shall never know if aliens live,
As I go home to Earth.

David Brown (10)
Our Lady And St Kenelm RC School

THE FOOTBALLER

I run out onto the pitch,
Tension running down my spine,
Will I score? The crowd is cheering -
I line up, ready to go.
Whistle blows, I'm off
Like a rocket going into space;
Down the wing I come, ready to tackle.
Wow! I've got the ball,
My fellow players cheering -
I'm getting closer . . . is that goalkeeper ready to save
My fabulous goal? Will the tough leather ball bounce
Out of his hands? Is he good enough?

I shall never know. Too soon my alarm clock goes off,
I'm back again, my regular bedroom.

Anna Toner (9)
Our Lady And St Kenelm RC School

THE METEOR

I start on Mars leaving the planet behind,
Flying through space like a cheetah through a desert.
The secrets of space along my blurring path,
On and on I go.
Over spacemen that look and point,
Over planets that disappear into the background.
Look, stars falling around me,
They go further when I try to reach them,
They're miles away . . .
Does that planet hold aliens that are in little green suits
With six eyes and four hands?
The alien empire?
What do they have?
Things called money, food and water?

I shall never know for too soon,
NASA sends a missile that breaks me into half,
Left goes to Venus, right goes to Mars.
Flying back to space I go,
Back home I go, back home where I come from,
The journey is over . . .

Rhiannon-Jayne Kilby (9)
Our Lady And St Kenelm RC School

THE TORNADO

Tornado is near,
I can hear,
Twisting and twirling,
Crashing and bashing,
Ripping and hitting,
People are:
Screaming and falling,
Calling, crying and whining,
My world is crumbling.

Sarah Towe (9)
Our Lady And St Kenelm RC School

THE DANCE SHOW

In the dressing room people are:
Giggling, whispering, chatting and nervous.

Leaping, prancing, pirouetting and dancing,
Altogether in a row - skipping, tapping,
Making a noise.

Tiptoeing, swirling, jumping and twirling,
Across the stage, tapping our feet,
Twisting and turning to the beat.

In the dressing room people are:
Giggling, whispering, chatting and relieved.

Rebecca Gower (10) & Emma Tierney (9)
Our Lady And St Kenelm RC School

BONFIRE NIGHT

November 5th is Bonfire Night,
Children eating and drinking,
Parents smacking, children crying.

Bonfire spitting and roaring,
The wood burning, children playing,
Parents yelling.

Fireworks banging and crackling,
Some screeching and soundless,
November 5th is Bonfire Night.

Jack Pickford (9)
Our Lady And St Kenelm RC School

THE ACTRESS

I put on my costume and prepare to act,
Getting ready like an impatient squirrel,
On the stage everything is set up,
This is my chance!
Playing dramatic and funny scenes.
I face the stage,
I see the cameras staring at me
And I remember nerves melt
And become someone for all to see . . .
I think of the specialities that my character has,
She is scary, naughty and sad,
But also happy, kind and funny,
Although she is mostly bad!

I wish it was true,
Too soon,
I am ready to go to the school play,
My 10-year-old body returns
And I walk on the stage to be Mary
In the Christmas play.

Dominique Birch (9) & Leah Olive (10)
Our Lady And St Kenelm RC School

THE PLAYGROUND

Noisy is the playground,
Children are:
Walking and talking,
Shouting and leaping,
Calling and falling,
Wondering and dashing,
Yelling and telling,
Whining and smiling,
Banging and smashing,
Thumping and bumping,
Skipping and tripping,
Running and spinning,
Flapping and clapping,
Bell is ringing,
Silent is the playground!

James Guy & Daniel Cleary (9)
Our Lady And St Kenelm RC School

NIGHT-TIME

In the woods there are;
Foxes slinking,
Owls flying,
Crickets jumping
And insects scuttling.

In the water there are;
Frogs leaping,
Fish darting,
Newts gliding
And deer drinking.

In the town there are;
Dogs barking,
Cats miaowing,
Babies crying
And people sleeping!

Emily Higgins (9)
Our Lady And St Kenelm RC School

TWIN POEM

There were some twins called Hannah and Heather,
Who always were together,
Even at school they were together,
Even at lunch they sat together,
Even at home they played together,
Apart, *never ever!*

Catherine Higgins & Jessica Willetts (8)
Our Lady And St Kenelm RC School

A WATER CYCLE POEM

It starts off when the sun sucks up the water from the sea,
No one can see it happen, but me.
It starts to make a cloud,
The cloud gets heavier and heavier, until it rains
And goes underground, I found,
It goes in rocks,
It goes in the river,
It goes back in the sea,
Then it stars all over again
And still no one can see, but me.

Esther Woaken (7)
Our Lady And St Kenelm RC School

THE SWIMMING POOL

In the swimming pool people are
Diving and splashing,
Racing and winning with each other,
Crying and yelling to their mother.
People dancing and prancing,
I'm getting out now,
My tummy is rumbling.

Jade Garner (9)
Our Lady And St Kenelm RC School

INSECTS

I   nsects are creepy crawlies
N   ot much are nice, most are gorys
S   ome are slimy, some are not
E   xtraordinary insects have stripes and spots
C   raneflies, beetles, moths and ants
T   iny ones fly round and get stuck in your pants.

David Grandey (10)
Perryfields J&I School

ANGELS IN THE CLOUDS

High up above in the clouds in the sky,
The angels sing heavenly songs,
They shout alleluia and make the sun shine,
They make it glow all the time.

God talks to them and makes them happy,
Their halos sparkle all day,
Their big white gowns hang off them,
They all gleam like a big white gem.

Then night comes and all goes dark,
But Heaven stays alight,
As the angels gleam,
Better than you could ever dream.

Amy Farndon (11)
Perryfields J&I School

I HATE EGGS

Mum said, 'Eggs for tea.'
I said, 'Yuk! No, not for me.'
She said, 'Yes, eggs for tea.'
I said, 'Yuk! No eggs for me.'

She put the eggs on my plate,
I said out loud, 'Eggs, I hate.'
Boiled, scrambled or fried,
Every kind of way I've tried.

I sat there eating up my tea,
'Yuk, eggs for tea.'
'Eat up all your eggs,' Mum said.
'Can I have some beans instead?'

Then one day I had my tea,
Mum said, 'Eggs for tea.'
I looked at my mum and began to cry,
Mum said, 'Okay, some beans we will try.'

Genna Haynes (9)
Perryfields J&I School

UNDERWATER WORLD

When the sun shines on the sea,
It shines like glitter.
When you hear the echo of dolphins,
It sounds like the song of the crickets.
When you see the fish of the sea,
They glide like the wind.
When you feel the soft sand beneath your feet,
It feels like your soft, furry teddy bear.
When the shells get washed up onto the beach,
It sounds like a multitude of people clapping.
When you're climbing the sand dunes on the beach,
It's like you're climbing forever and ever.
When your ice cream is dripping down your arm,
It feels like a snake wrapping round it.

Laura Shepherd (11)
Perryfields J&I School

THE CLASSROOM OF CHAOS!

Right children, it's time for a test,
Oh Peter, go away, you can be such a pest.
Do I hear talking at the back?
I'm really disappointed in you, Jack.
And who is that messing around with their chair?
Perhaps it might be Suzanne or Claire.
Do I see a ball?
That's not like you, Paul!

Louise Moran (10)
Perryfields J&I School

PETS

Pets are meant for loving,
Pets are meant for enjoyment and happiness,
Pets are meant for me!

Pets are meant for playing ball,
Pets are meant for taking walkies,
Pets are meant for me!

Pets are meant for taking care of,
Pets are meant to be our friends,
Pets are meant for me!

Grace Dashey (10)
Perryfields J&I School

HIDDEN TREASURES

My life is full of hidden treasures
My mum, my dad, my brother
My nan and granddad
My aunts and uncles
My mates too
And my pets, to name a few
My priceless treasures
Are my pleasures.

Scott Gibson (11)
Perryfields J&I School

MY CAT HAS A FEVER

My cat feels very hot,
I think it's because he's eaten a lot.
He's been in gardens and all around,
He's even been to places that are out of bounds.
He's eaten mice and nibbled birds,
But still out his mouth came no words.
He's looked for worms and searched for a beaver
And do you know what?
My cat has a fever!

Rebecca Jukes (10)
Perryfields J&I School

HIDDEN TREASURES

Golden treasure hidden somewhere
Pirates looking everywhere
Where could the treasure be?
Under sand?
Under sea?

Where could the treasure be?
Easy to find
Hard to find
Probably somewhere hard to find
Where is the box that's filled with treasure?
Probably somewhere filled with pleasure

A pirate saw something special
But it wasn't any treasure
Everybody is going crazy
Looking for the hidden treasure.

Luke Rainsford (8)
Perryfields J&I School

THE SECRET KEY

Look into the deep blue sea,
There you will find a secret key.
The key unlocks a world full of treasure,
That sparkles and glistens for your pleasure.
A diamond ring for you to wear,
With coloured gems to put in your hair.
You too could be lucky enough to wear,
These things that are so very rare.
So take a look into the sea
And hope you will find the secret key.

Kate Shropshall (10)
Perryfields J&I School

MY LITTLE SISTER

Crawling along the floor
Towards the open door

Onto the landing, she doesn't get far
We're close behind but show her a toy car

She starts to laugh and giggle
And starts to crawl back to the middle
On the landing

She's my little treasure
She's my little sister.

Francesca Williams (11)
Perryfields J&I School

THE GIBLINGS

Upon the hill where the night is bold;
Stories are swapped and secrets are told.
Young giblings play,
Older ones pray.
While the middlers gossip and chat away;
As the clock strikes midnight, eyes look high,
But the magic passes with a sigh
And the next full moon, eyes will wait,
To see if the magic comes and opens the gate,
But now they'll have to wait.
The giblings wait year after year,
But the gibling magic never comes.
They wait, they wait to see their fate,
Will they become human?
Upon the hill where the night is bold,
Stories are swapped and secrets are told.
The giblings are always there in front of the gate,
That is where they wait, they wait.

Rachel Moran (10)
Perryfields J&I School

HIDDEN TREASURE

Pirates, pirates,
Lovely treasure,
Lost it, lost it,
Now all gone.

Treasure, treasure,
Now it is found,
Home again, home again,
Homeward bound.

Pirates, pirates,
They are glad,
Gold, gold,
It's not so bad.

Treasure, treasure,
A golden surprise,
Rich, rich,
Golden as the sunrise.

Pirates, pirates,
Lovely treasure,
Hidden it, hidden it,
Now all gone.

Treasure, treasure,
A treasure chest,
Hidden deep below,
In the sea.

Pirates, pirates,
They cannot find,
The hidden treasure,
That I have found.

Charlotte Abbotts (9)
Perryfields J&I School

LIFE

Life begins each morning,
Ever dawning,
It ends when you start sleeping,
Shadows creeping,
A new life will begin each day,
New things to do,
New things to say,
Life begins each morning,
Ever dawning.

Jennifer Weston (8)
Perryfields J&I School

KARATE FIGHT

I went to karate the other night
I stood there ready for the big fight
As I took a kick at the opposition
My foot went off in a strange position
All I remember is a great bright light
As I lay in hospital that night
I was always good at karate hits
But now I'm the best at doing the splits.

Ben White (11)
Perryfields J&I School

UNDER THE SEA

With coral of pink, red, yellow and white
And the water so blue, it's a wonderful sight.
Where fishes swim without a care in the world
And scientists go to discover a new world.

There are big fish and small fish in all sorts of colours,
That swim around for hours and hours.
Then you have the leggy octopus, but my favourite of all
Is the dolphin, the way it jumps and curls like a ball.

Beware of the whale and the shark that are down there
And take care not to be caught by its evil stare,
Because in a moment you will not be there.

Michael Floyd (11)
Perryfields J&I School

WHEN I WAS A GIRL

One Christmas when I was a little girl
I had a doll with a golden curl
She wore a dress and bonnet that was pretty and green
And she was the prettiest doll I'd ever seen
I called her Bethany, I bathed her and put her to bed
She had a bottle that emptied when she was fed

When I was a little girl aged about one
I had a teddy who was soft and cuddly
When I took her to bed
I thought and thought
Then I remembered her name was Winifred.

Grace Pemberton (9)
Perryfields J&I School

NATURE WORLD

Daisies are white with honey in the middle,
Buttercups are made of butter,
Which make their petals very yellow.
Birds are grey with lovely, long feathers,
Chicks chirp hungrily waiting for their mother to bring worms.
This is what I call a nature world!

Sadeh Gayle (10)
Perryfields J&I School

PUPPIES AND DOGS!

Puppies and dogs are cute in every way,
I could stroke them and stroke them day after day.
I would stroke them and pat them and tickle their tum,
I would like to take them out for their little run.
Oh, I do love dogs and puppies, oh puppies,
But I really like Huskies, oh Huskies, they're lovely.
I would do anything for a puppy or a dog,
I would take them out, even for a jog.
If only there was a fairy to grant me this wish,
Because all I have got now are two little fish!

Emily Floyd (9)
Perryfields J&I School

MY GOLDEN FOOTBALL

'I'm bored,' I said to my mum one day,
While she was digging in the garden.
'Why don't you just go and play
Or try cleaning out the shed.'

I ran up to the garden shed
And took out all the rubbish,
My mum shouted, 'Mind the flowerbed,'
As all the tools were scattered.

I cleaned and swept with a brush,
Then I saw something glistening,
I was then in such a rush
And I almost fell over.

I couldn't believe my eyes,
In amongst the tools,
But it was then, to my surprise,
It was a brilliant, golden football!

Matthew McDonough (10)
Perryfields J&I School

CARS

I love most cars
At a hundred miles or two
One day they will go to Mars
Looking like a comet, golden and blue

I wish I had a car for me
Sparkling gold with all the frills
When I get one it will be for thee
And I hope in the winter, it doesn't get the chills.

Frankie Heard (10)
Perryfields J&I School

SPACEMAN

I'd like to be a spaceman
And travel to the stars
Investigating planets such as Jupiter and Mars.

I'd hope to meet an alien
Who would invite me to dinner
But I don't think I'd like their food
And end up much thinner

I'd bring him back to Earth
And introduce him to my friends
I'd go down in the history books
As someone rather clever
People would look at me and point at me
And say, 'Look, there's that fella.'

Liam Hill (10)
Perryfields J&I School

GOLDEN GLORY

H   ey matey, what can we find?
I   don't know Captain
D   ig deep, my boy
D   on't worry, I will Captain
E   nough, that's enough, stop digging
N   ow what do I do, Captain?

T   ake the chest out
R   ight-o Captain
E   mpty it
A   ll right Captain
S   hift out my way and let me see
U   nless I'm mistaken, it's empty
R   each in deeper
E   ureka! We've found the golden glory.

Joe Clarke (10)
Perryfields J&I School

THE VAULTS

There is an underground bank for wizards
It has horrible-looking goblin guards
With outside decorations of stone gargoyles
And walls made out of marble
Wizards go up to the desks to get a key
So they can enter the vaults for their money
Some wizards say those goblin guards look strange
They are there to look after your change
In the cart, they begin to go fast
Down here, the place is so vast
Finally when a wizard gets to his vault
The cart slows down and comes to a halt
Just as well because by now everyone feels sick
Into the money-filled vault they take their pick
In vault 701 it would seem there is nothing there
The banker can only feel thin air
He reaches for the corner and lets out a moan
Oh! There is something there, it's the Philosopher's Stone.

Charlotte Draper (11)
Perryfields J&I School

HIDDEN TREASURES

Under the sea
There are secrets untold
Treasures and mermaids and a city of gold

Where diamonds sparkle like
Stars in the night and in the day
A ruby sun shines ever so bright

Under the sea-world where mermaids play
Making strings of pearls they sing away
Under the sea, no one would ever know

This world of hidden treasure
Down there below.

Lydia Hughes (10)
Perryfields J&I School

My Mum And Dad

My mum really wants me to try,
To get good marks and reach for the sky.

I try my best, I really do,
I hope that works when the marks come through.

My mum promised to get me a treat,
Some nice Rockports to fit my feet.

I came home from rugby one night,
Plastered in mud, oh what a sight.

Rugby's the game for real hard men,
That's why me and my dad go time and time again.

Jack Baker (10)
Perryfields J&I School

HIDDEN TREASURE

When a rainbow shines on the Earth,
There is always treasure there,
But where?
Find it if you dare.
Pirates' treasure under the sand,
They buried it with their own hands.
'I've found it!' said a person over there,
But there will always be another one,
But where?
Find it if you dare.

Selina Barrett (11)
Perryfields J&I School

HIDDEN TREASURES

Down in the deep blue sea,
There are lots of hidden treasures for you and me.
You see how they shimmer and shine,
Oh! I wish they could all be mine.
The pearls shine oh so brightly,
The diamonds fit in oh so delightedly.
There are about a thousand-and-seven,
There are red jewels
And there are blue jewels,
But they are all hidden treasures in the sea,
Lots of them but not for you and me.

Rebekah Jones (10)
Perryfields J&I School

THE FOREST

I go camping every year in the wood!
Tonight is the night,
The wood is creeping upon me,
I hear hoots and howls,
Fear runs down my spine.

In my tent, I see a shadow,
It looks like a bear growling at me,
Panic, panic, scream,
Is it my imagination running riot again?

The moon shines down on the wet grass,
The grass looked like glass in the moonlight,
I see a light, I run towards it,
It is my dad, he takes me home
And still every night,
Hoots and howls!

Abbey-May Darbey (9)
St Paul's CE Primary School, Wolverhampton

THE FOREST

In the forest,
The darkness is looming over me.
Red flowers turn black,
Squeals from all over.
A big shadow,
I look down, there's a rat!
The trees suddenly turn into people,
I can make out the face.
The adrenalin rushes through my body,
Like a river it flows along.
A branch cracked,
I spin around but there's nothing.
There is an owl hooting,
My imagination is running wild!
A bat flits above my head,
I scream, the sound echoes.
I see something that makes my heart stop,
There's a bright light.
I run to follow the light,
There's a woodcutter's hut.
I knock on the door,
A gruff man with a beard answers.
He looks scary but his face breaks into a smile.
He gives me a bed,
The forest howls behind me.

Kirsten Eagle
St Paul's CE Primary School, Wolverhampton

THE FOREST

In a moonlit forest a hooting grew louder,
A twig cracked,
The trees closed in on me,
Like a trap where walls move in.

Leaves whisper while squirrels scurry up trees,
The rain beats the ground, the clouds keep going darker and darker,
The thunder and lightning starts,
Then a light,
It was a house,
I ran to safety.

Shreece Dennis-Beecher
St Paul's CE Primary School, Wolverhampton

THE FOREST

Walking through the forest,
It was getting dark,
Lots of rustling could be heard,
I was getting scared.

Suddenly a wolf jumped out,
I began to run away,
Still I ran and still it chased,
But I managed to lose it.

Now I am lost,
I start to cry,
I shout, 'Help! Help!'
No one comes to help.

Some light I see,
'Alleluia,' I shout,
I run towards it,
The sun it was.

Home I found,
Knock, knock, the door banged,
Door opens,
In I run.

Mum hugged me,
Happy I was,
I fell on the carpet, exhausted,
I was safe.

Stephen Williams (9)
St Paul's CE Primary School, Wolverhampton

THE FOREST

The moon shines on everything like a shining star,
Rustling noises, what's that on the ground?
Oh good, only a badger looking for food,
What's that noise?

Trees looking like ghosts and monsters,
Owls are hooting,
Bats are swooping,
Nearly everything's moving.

Running quickly,
I hear other noises,
I run even faster and faster,
Tripping over a tree's root sticking out of the ground.

Big tears roll down my face,
I know I'm far away from home,
Sadness within now fills me,
I scream out loud so someone can hear me,
But no one calls back.

Then silence, total silence,
Fear runs down my spine,
Panic grows within me,
Suddenly I see a light.

Just standing there out of the blue,
Stood a house,
I run inside and see a nice, warm place.

Chelsey Fairfax (10)
St Paul's CE Primary School, Wolverhampton

THE FOREST

It was now getting late in the forest,
Darkness was flooding the ground.
Tree branches were looking like long, bony witch fingers,
Every little sound was drowned by silence.

Hedges were looking like trolls, the moon had grown eyes,
Bats were screeching like alarm bells,
Owls were pouncing on prey.

A shuffling hedgehog looked like a pin cushion,
The long grass felt like furry snakes.
Fox dens looked like caves,
Molehills were looking like cliffs.

The wind was painted by the leaves as they fluttered and swooped,
Lightning lit the sky,
The thunder bellowed, trembling the ground.
The wind howled,
Then everything went silent again.

Everything was still, there wasn't even a twitch,
Things seemed scary again,
Run, don't go in,
The forest isn't a nice place,
So, don't go in!

Hannah Phillips (9)
St Paul's CE Primary School, Wolverhampton

THE FOREST

The forest
I see birds flying in the air
Trees waving from the wind
The sun shining in my eyes

The forest
Closer and closer the sun goes down
The grass gets shorter
Trees begging to go to the ground

The forest
I'll come when the sun appears
It goes darker and darker
Now I see a house

Out to the forest
Nice in the daytime
Time to go home

Out to the forest
I lost my way
Just follow these footprints
Then to get to my home

Out of the forest
I'm out finally
The sun is out to shine
I'm going home

Out of the forest
The birds are flying in the air
I can see hills and mountains
I can hear people calling

To my home
My home at last
I see the smoke from the kettle
I hear the spoon clanging

To bed
Goodnight I said
Till morning rises.

Terri Ellis
St Paul's CE Primary School, Wolverhampton

THE FOREST

The forest, what a wonderful place,
The flowers, the crispy leaves that fall.
The moon that glows all night,
The trees reshape and look like faces.

Owls hoot as they fly across the night sky,
Hedgehogs that scurry across the ground.
Rabbits hopping along the path,
There is silence all around.

The wind blowing the trees,
The flowers and the leaves,
The sky's gone dark now,
It's dark everywhere I look.

I'm scared, all on my own,
There's no one around at all.
Suddenly a bright light,
I am found.

Amy Morgan (10)
St Paul's CE Primary School, Wolverhampton

THE FOREST

Through the forest the brothers walked
As Phil and Pete walked through autumn leaves
Saw a movement did Phil
Said to run as night had fallen
They didn't know where to go
Pete had dropped the compass
Phil was scared, he didn't know what the creature was
Pete asked where the movement came from
Then Pete shone the light around
And to their surprise was a lizard
Looking for scraps, worms or ants
Then they agreed to go home
But lost the compass
Then a call came
It was their parents, shouting for their children
The children followed and came home once more
Never to go in the forest again.

Jamie Fairhurst
St Paul's CE Primary School, Wolverhampton

THE FOREST

I'm in the forest going camping
I need to set up the tent
And set out the fire and beds
I say to myself, I'll get the sticks

So I go off looking for some sticks
I get the sticks and then lose my way
It is getting darker, I'm terrified
Twigs snapping, voices echoing
Owls hooting, trees give me spooky looks

The heavy wind blows against me
I run with fear in any direction
Then I find a house with the door open
I walk in and say, 'Hello.' Nobody answers
Then a man walks in and says,
'Hello, what are you doing here?'

I tell him I've lost my way,
This was the nearest place,
Can I stay?
The man puts the fire on
And it's warm.

Danielle Fannell (9)
St Paul's CE Primary School, Wolverhampton

THE FOREST

Moonlight fell on the forest floor,
Where trees tried to grab you as you ran.
A howling gale tried to stop you running.
Panic struck you!
Something was lurching in the forest,
You tripped,
But you couldn't see what you tripped over.
The stars were as sparkling as diamonds.
Then you saw a light,
You didn't dare to look through.
Owls hooted wildly as they called to their friends
And you ran towards the light.
Then you came to a large house,
You were safe!
You calmed down!

Aimee Westwood (10)
St Paul's CE Primary School, Wolverhampton

MY LITTLE DOG

My little puppy called Tucker
You would think he was quite a looker
But he's so blind
I go out of my mind
When a cat sits right in front of him

Tucker is so cuddly
But urgh! He is so muddy
He needs a bath
But what a laugh
We ended up wet instead of the puppy!

At night-time he sleeps in the kitchen
But he's so scared, what a chicken!
He is sweet
So I took a seat
And we fell asleep together.

Natasha Wolverson (11)
St Paul's CE Primary School, Wolverhampton

DEEP BLUE SEA

In I go, into the deep blue sea,
In my fish-shaped submarine.
Down, down I swiftly go,
Where seaweed grows and fish swim.

When I get down to the deepest part,
Low and behold! What do I see?
A chest of red,
Filled with gold jewels.

Then out comes a purple octopus,
With long, purple tentacles,
He grabs me and takes me deeper,
I'm stuck! I'm stuck! I'm stuck!

Suddenly I have a crazy idea!
My hands are ready to work,
I put the speed on to full blast
And go as fast as I can.

I grabbed the treasure with my strong ropes
And sped off to the surface.
'I'm rich,' I cried, 'I'm rich, rich, rich
And I found it in the sea.'

From that day on,
I was famous
For finding treasure in the sea.
Oh isn't it a glorious thing?
I didn't even earn it.

Jennifer Manders (10)
St Paul's CE Primary School, Wolverhampton

BRONX, BUNTY, MONTY AND JUKE

Bronx is my best friend,
He is also my dog,
We run together,
Knowing we're alone at home.
I could never, ever have a better friend,
We watch a movie together and fall asleep near the end.
He throws my toys and catches them again,
He's my bestest friend ever.
Monty is also my best friend,
He is doggy number two,
He was only 18 months when he left me,
I know he's still in Heaven but he still looks down on me.
Bunty is Monty's mummy,
She loved him so,
She too had cancer and had to go,
Bye-bye Bunty, I love you so.
Juke watched me when I played outside,
He used to give me rides on his back,
He was cuddly and funny,
I loved to play with him,
I miss them all a lot.

Alex Edmonds (10)
St Paul's CE Primary School, Wolverhampton

CARS

Cars, cars zooming, speeding cars
Going so fast you can't even see them

Cars, cars flashy, shiny cars
Showing off their gleaming coats

Cars, cars, there are so many
Which one to choose? I don't know

Cars, cars, look at that car
Big and small, I like them all

Cars, cars, all different colours
Red, green, black, blue too

Cars, cars, I really like that one
It's red, it's fast, it's the best!

Tashon Reid-Palmer (11)
St Paul's CE Primary School, Wolverhampton

BOOMING FIREWORKS

Boom, boom
   Booming fireworks
Booming fireworks flying off the ground
Beside me are children dancing around
Fireworks are fun and loud
Boom, boom, boom
   Booming fireworks
The lovely sparkle up in the sky
To not have fireworks makes me cry
Sparkling sparklers spelling out your name
Boom, boom
   Booming fireworks
Rockets, Catherine wheels
And other fireworks too
As they reach the sky, they separate and die
Boom, boom, boom
   Bang!

Lauren Bailey (11)
St Paul's CE Primary School, Wolverhampton

SUMMER

The sun shines down and on my face
I look up and the clouds look like space
I see people playing in a park
I hear the birds singing in a tree
Sweetly chirping at me

Now it's summer, I'm very happy
I went in some sand and got messy
I got out and I laid on the grass
When I went on the path, it almost burned my feet
There were a lot of people around me that I could meet

No rain came by me whatsoever
Me and my friends would play together
The summer was coming to an end
Fun can't last forever you know!
So summer will soon start to go

It was great while it lasted this year
Now autumn is coming near
The sun starts to go down
But winter will come with rain and snow
All the seasons will come and go.

Victoria Smith (10)
St Paul's CE Primary School, Wolverhampton

PETS

There are lots of pets
In the world,
So go down and buy one
And you better trust them all.

I've got a pet,
He is so small,
I brought him
In a big pet stall.

My cousin's pet
Is a dog,
That's lovely,
Warm and sweet.

There are lots of pets
To choose from,
So choose the one
That fits you the most.

My pet's a rabbit,
He's got furry feet,
My friend loves him
And I think he's sweet.

I love my pet called Thumper
And I never leave him alone,
My mum always tells me off,
Having him in the home.

I called my rabbit Thumper
Because he thumps in his home.

Natalie Purcell (11)
St Paul's CE Primary School, Wolverhampton

SEASONS

Autumn leaves collide, softly to the ground,
It makes my head whirl around.
As I see the bare trees,
The stars begin to glisten down on me.

As autumn sets aside, winter begins,
With snow falling up from the rooftops.
Birds no longer sing as the land is cold,
My heart turns to ice as if the world around me was stone-cold.

Spring begins with chirping birds,
My heart singing out to the world.
Flowers spring into the air,
As I feel the breeze in my hair,
A song is in my heart for summer is near.

Summertime is time for indulging in ice cream
And going on shopping sprees.
Summertime means parties for me,
For August the thirteenth is my birthday
And celebrate shall we.

The seasons are changing time after time,
As they move so quickly we shall enjoy the nature
And scenery that only god can have created,
For all to see!

Sophia Thandi (10)
St Paul's CE Primary School, Wolverhampton

WIND

The wind is as bold as the midnight moon
Wind is as pure as water from a rippling brook
Wind is as precious as gold

Air is needed to keep our organs working
Air, there is none that we do not need
In space, air is a dream that will never come true

Wind is invisible to the human eye
Wind is never detected, only felt
Wind is always used

Air can be hot or cold
Air can be strong or thin
Air and wind will never stop.

Josh Pillinger (10)
St Paul's CE Primary School, Wolverhampton

BLOOD

Blood is red
Blood is hate
Blood makes people mad
Blood is anger
Blood is war
Blood is pain
Blood is ferocious
Blood is death
Blood can kill.

Michael Jones (11)
St Paul's CE Primary School, Wolverhampton

THE SUN

I can burn people and scratch the Earth
Or gently warm the Earth
And help to open flowers
In summertime I'm out all day
In winter I'm only out at play
But either way I'm always there
Behind the clouds or in the air.

Laura Collins (9)
St Nicholas' RC Primary School, Sutton Coldfield

AIR SHOW

Children watch, children stare
As the planes fly in the air
They rise and fall, turn and jive
Best of all they flip and dive
At the end, people agree it was fine
I agree, I'll come back anytime.

Joe Martin (10)
St Nicholas' RC Primary School, Sutton Coldfield

LIVING

Seeing the beauty of a single flower,
That is the elegance of living.
Hearing the splutter of a babbling brook,
That is the beauty of living.
Appreciating that sunset isn't just the end of a day,
That is the truth of living.
Caring for one another,
That is the love of living.
Knowing that every second of every day is precious,
That is truly living.

Ellie Jurczak (10)
St Nicholas' RC Primary School, Sutton Coldfield

SPACE

Space is a very strange place,
It can never hide.
It can never get bigger or smaller,
It goes on forever.

Space is a very strange place,
There is more to it than we can see.
It would take millions of years to go round it,
It goes on forever
        and ever
            and ever
                and ever,
Until the end of the world.

Jennifer Millman (11)
St Nicholas' RC Primary School, Sutton Coldfield

SILHOUETTE STRANGER

S lowly moving in the distance
I ndividual, creeping secretly
L ord of the shadows arrives
H e lurks alone
O n his own two feet
U nder and over
E verywhere is covered
T reetops lie still
T rembling as he runs
E verybody lies asleep

S o quietly, not a sound is heard
T hrough the streets
R ound the corners
A rriving soon is the morning
N ever will he be caught
G reat fear dawns upon the world
E ven though the street is sleeping
R unning before the sun arrives.

Rebecca Breen (11)
St Nicholas' RC Primary School, Sutton Coldfield

GOING TO GRANDMA'S FOR SUNDAY LUNCH

It's Sunday lunch at Grandma's house,
Lumpy gravy and Brussels sprouts.
My tummy somersaults at the thought,
I haven't even finished my first course!

Cold turkey and soggy carrots,
I'm surprised Grandma's oven doesn't have maggots.
My sister disappears for a while
And then appears with a pale weak smile.

Yellow cake which is falling apart,
My gran describes it as apple tart.
Custard that tastes like tea,
This has been a bad day for me.

Grainne Reihill (10)
St Nicholas' RC Primary School, Sutton Coldfield

GEORGE

I know today won't be any different,
To the week before or the week before that,
So I put on my gloves and tighten my riding hat.

My instructor will say, 'You'll be riding today . . .'
And I'll think, 'Please not George,' in my head,
Yet I hear, 'Go get George, go ahead.'

I unlock the stable door angrily feeling so annoyed,
I could throw it right into the dirt,
But when I step in and see George's face,
He looks so knowing and hurt.

He seems to know what I'm thinking
And I wish I didn't think it anymore.
I give him a quick hug and
Lead him out of the stable door.

I take him out in the field
And get him sorted out,
He'll misbehave as usual,
In that there is no doubt.

At first George is excited
And wants to trot around,
But then he starts ignoring me
And stands still on the ground.

I don't want to hurt George,
Because I'd feel so cruel,
Even though, with him
I can never keep my cool.

Though he's a pain sometimes
And makes me really mad,
If I ever couldn't ride him,
I'd be very sad!

Celia Taylor (10)
St Nicholas' RC Primary School, Sutton Coldfield

FIRE; THE DEPRESSOR

Fire.
Hot sparks,
Shoot at anything.
Burns and causes dreadful
Pain.

Fire,
It dominates.
Pierces your heart.
You wish it would
Leave.

Fire.
Traps you,
Terrifies, hurts you.
It won't let you
Go.

Fire.
A lion,
Roars at you.
Massive jaws covered in
Destruction.

Fire.
Follows you
And traps you,
In its path of
Evil.

Fire.
It's stopped.
We are safe.
We can live life
Again.

Christopher Kimmet (11)
St Nicholas' RC Primary School, Sutton Coldfield

STAR WONDER

I wonder what's on a star,
Maybe a vehicle like my car
Or maybe something incredibly hairy
Or maybe something that's terribly scary!
I wonder, I wonder.

On this star which is afar,
It shines all so very bright.
Maybe it has many lamps alight,
To give us such a wonderful picture,
I wonder, I wonder.

Every night before I sleep,
I gaze into the lights so bright,
Through the maze of all the stars,
To find my friend to say goodnight.

Ciara McBrine (10)
St Nicholas' RC Primary School, Sutton Coldfield

PARADISE

The cool turquoise liquid drifts across my toes,
As I walk on a bed of beige diamonds.
The rounded palms sway
And the light, cheerful breeze dances through my hair.
This is my true paradise.

Hannah Reaney-Dickinson (10)
St Nicholas' RC Primary School, Sutton Coldfield

CHAIR

The chair was so straight, so dark, so strong,
It made me feel warm like a fire burning through my body.
No one knew my chair but all I said was see to believe
And that's what I did.
I trusted my chair and told it all my secrets.
My chair was my friend to whom I told all my wishes.
People laugh and mock my chair,
But he's my friend until the end.

Katie Sexton (11)
St Nicholas' RC Primary School, Sutton Coldfield

THE SUN

The sun rose slowly,
gradually the city filled with light,
the sun smiled at all the people,
it waved its rays of light around.

The sun is everyone's friend,
he has no enemies,
no one is left in darkness when he's around,
no one is left out.

The sun waved goodbye
and smiled one last time,
slowly, the city filled with darkness,
as the sun began to set.

Grainne Coombs (10)
St Nicholas' RC Primary School, Sutton Coldfield

SUNRISE SURPRISE!

As the sun comes out to play,
Who do you think will rule the day?
His rays shine down on the grass,
The warmth of his people in his grasp.

His smile is warm, big and free,
People who see him shout with glee.
But tomorrow's great morning rise,
Will be the best of the sunrise surprise.

Katie Shanahan (10)
St Nicholas' RC Primary School, Sutton Coldfield

THE DEVIL

The Devil seems to chase,
All that is in his view,
No one could survive!

He ran after screaming people,
He banished those who asked for mercy,
He cackled as his tail beat.

Then God showed up,
With a trident and a spear,
Banishing the Devil to the underworld.

Leanne Gallagher (10)
St Nicholas' RC Primary School, Sutton Coldfield

FIRE

In the morning we could see it,
Hugging the whole forest.
Later that day,
It ate the house.
The house that housed the dogs.
I think the worst it's ever done,
Is scare my little sister.
Does it even have a heart?
This scary, fiery fire.

Rebecca Lewis (10)
St Nicholas' RC Primary School, Sutton Coldfield

THE IT

It's creeping by my bedside
And underneath my pillow.
It's coming up, does it bite? Will it strangle me?
That little thing I hate to see creeping by me.
I'm watching to see if it's there.
Morn is here, it's time to see what damage it has done.
Under my pillow is a golden pound coin,
Sitting there for me.
Maybe that thing by my bedside is kind, just maybe.

Kim Lawrence (10)
St Nicholas' RC Primary School, Sutton Coldfield

FROST

Jack Frost is a mischievous child,
Leaving trouble behind him.
As he dances past lamp posts and houses,
He leaves a trail of glitter behind him.

It is as if he is freezing time,
Whatever he touches turns to ice.
His sharp eyes dart here and there,
To survey his wondrous work.

Jack Frost never rests,
With little feelings for anyone.
I wonder if his heart is as cold as his play?

Emily Liggins (11)
St Nicholas' RC Primary School, Sutton Coldfield

MIST

He creeps around like a robber,
Surrounding the house.
Waiting for the right moment.
He's the predator and his victim is the prey.
Confusing people, throwing them off their path.
He's ready when you're on your own,
No one to protect you!

Heart beating faster, you start to run,
Bump-bump, bump-bump.
You can't escape his vaporous hands,
You feel damp, deadly coldness enfold your body.
He's a thief who wants to take your joy,
He's ready when you're on your own,
No one to protect you!

Elliot Geddes (10)
St Nicholas' RC Primary School, Sutton Coldfield

RAIN

On dark, cold, misty nights
The rain bursts from its house
In the clouds
It dives down onto the unknown territory
Or slides down roofs
Then it slithers along the ground
While the rest of the followers
Fly with the wind
And knock on every window and door
When the clouds break
And the mist clears
The sun will rise and pull the rain back
Exhausted to its home.

Joseph Killian (10)
St Nicholas' RC Primary School, Sutton Coldfield

WHY? WHY?

He said for me to do it
But I didn't want to
He said he'd pay me
But I knew that wasn't true

I made my way there
And stood still
How could I do this?
It was against my will

Now today as I sit
As I sit in my prison cell
No one will know
Because I won't tell.

Philippa Harwood (11)
St Nicholas' RC Primary School, Sutton Coldfield

DON'T BE CRUEL TO ANIMALS

Don't be cruel to animals,
they are truly, your best friends.
Sure, they can be a little strange,
but have been with you through odds and ends.

Don't be cruel to animals,
whether they're tame or wild.
All they want is a little love,
so treat them like your own child.

So don't be cruel to animals,
if they ruin the furniture with their claws
or even if they walk in the house
with dirty, muddy paws.

But animals are our mates you see
and all they need is some TLC!

Kirsten Kimmet (11)
St Nicholas' RC Primary School, Sutton Coldfield

THE CREATURE!

Sweeping through the forest,
Comes to a halt,
Knocks on the window, no answer,
So it climbs down the chimney
With hairy feet,
Down . . . down . . . slips!

Jade Clark (11)
St Nicholas' RC Primary School, Sutton Coldfield

ROBIN

Little robin redbreast sits in the tree,
Singing very loud.
Hiding in the bushes, a fluffy coat,
Waiting to pounce.
Other birds give a warning,
All fly away into the distance,
The cat walks away, to try again later.

Alex Winter (10)
St Nicholas' RC Primary School, Sutton Coldfield

MY MUM AND DAD

My mum and dad are really mad,
They're bonkers all day long
And when it's time to go to bed,
They sing a 60s song.

My mum and dad are really mad,
My dad wears his trousers so high,
My mum wears bright pink tops
And they think they can fly.

My mum and dad are really mad,
But I think you'll agree,
I love my mum and dad
And they love me.

Joanna Maguire (10)
St Nicholas' RC Primary School, Sutton Coldfield

CREATURES OF THE NIGHT

A nimals creeping out at night,
R ummaging in the undergrowth, looking for tasty plants,
M aking it hard for predators with its horn-capped plates,
A s silently as they can, they dig their burrows safely under
the ground,
D iving away from enemies into the warm earth,
I nvertebrates everywhere unknowing they're its prey,
L iving safely, finding food in the ground,
L eaving a dirt track wherever they go,
O pening eyes when they hear a noise,
S o what are they?

Connor Martin (9)
St Nicholas' RC Primary School, Sutton Coldfield

BONFIRE NIGHT

Embers drifting off into the midnight sky,
Children playing with sparkling sticks,
Rockets, Catherine wheels, roman candles,
All exploding in a mix of colours,
The glow of people's faces watching this neat display,
The wail of the tall rockets blasting into clouds,
To make an umbrella of shimmering light,
The sound of amazement from the children's voices,
Oh, what a night it's been.

Matthew Cotter (9)
St Nicholas' RC Primary School, Sutton Coldfield

COLOURS

Red as a crisp leaf on a tree
Yellow as mild honey from a bee

Pink as a petal shining bright
Orange is always in sight

Blue as the clear crystal sea
Green as a frozen pea

Purple as the coat I wear
Brown as a big, fuzzy bear

Silver as the midnight sky
Gold as a crusty pie

White as a swan swimming past
Black as brand new shoes, nice and fast.

Victoria Stones (10)
St Nicholas' RC Primary School, Sutton Coldfield

THE BOY WAS MAD

There was a boy who was chocolate mad
He was always actin' bad

He had a brother who was so, so silly
He had a dog that was called Billy

He was always buying stuff
His brother eats cheesy puffs.

Jack Fisher (9)
Tividale Hall Primary School

STRAIGHT SOCCER!

I was in a soccer team,
We kicked the ball on a beam,
That's why we were called the
Straight Soccer team.

When I quit,
My uncle fell down a pit,
So I went back on the
Straight soccer team,
To make him proud.

Now I am twenty-two,
I am Michael Owen number two,
Now David Beckham is jealous of me,
Because I can kick a ball at a bumblebee.

Now in my old age,
I only read books page by page,
It is really sad,
I wish I still had my mum and dad.

Now I cry,
My eyes sizzle and fry,
I still want my mum and dad,
I know it is really *sad!*

Anthony Shipley (9)
Tividale Hall Primary School

THE QUEEN LIVES AT BUCKINGHAM PALACE

I saw the Queen at Buckingham Palace
And she hates the name Alice.

She saw a little diamond ring
And she saw it with the king.

She was sitting all day on her throne,
Feeling the precious stone.

She looked up to the stars
And she saw the planet Mars.

She hates it when somebody's name is Alice,
Because she lives in Buckingham Palace.

Manpreet Dhillon (9)
Tividale Hall Primary School

I LIKE ART

I like art,
It's really cool.
I love painting,
Only I wish it could be better.
I like drawing,
Collages too!
I like making things from plastic,
It's easy to bend.
Different shades make a good picture,
Different textures on your paper.
I like drawing jungles,
Especially monkeys and snakes.
My friends like art,
I do too,
But I want to know if you do?

Rhea Asfaw (9)
Tividale Hall Primary School

STARS AND THE NIGHT

Stars, stars, in the moonlight,
Twinkling in the dark,
The black sky holding back the morning light,
Where is the sun hiding?
Behind the blanket of darkness.

Here comes the morning,
So let's all rise and shine,
To welcome the new day,
Let's hope everyone's fine.

Ryan Howells (8)
Tividale Hall Primary School

WHEN I PLAYED FOR THE FOOTBALL TEAM

When I played for a football team,
I scored a million goals.
The player on the other team,
Made a million fouls.
I took my shot, I hit the pole,
Scholes came in and scored the goal.

Jack Moore (9)
Tividale Hall Primary School

MY USUAL DAY AT SCHOOL

First lesson at my school is maths,
We have to be careful in PE, so we sit on mats.
Some people at my school like art,
The naughty children have to be kept apart.
I get up in the morning, look forward to seeing my mates,
But when I realise the time, I know I'm going to be late.
I get dressed in a mess, rush off to school,
My teacher is standing there, like I've broken the law.
She tells me I've got to miss my play for a whole week,
But worse than that, I've got to mend the school leak.
So I go and do my job,
Then on my way home, go to the shop.

Michelle Humphrey (8)
Tividale Hall Primary School

THE DAY THE DINOSAUR CAME TO SCHOOL!

A dinosaur walked up the lane,
Dressed in a pinafore, black and white,
It's really such a funny sight.

He made a big, gigantic hole,
Through the headmaster's room,
He made the Year 5 teachers run away to sea!
The dinosaur ate a pot of toadstool stew,
Which made the school say yippee!
But the nursery kids just cried, waw, waw,
That's the tale of the dinosaur who came to school!

Emily Gates (9)
Tividale Hall Primary School

ANIMALS

I'm a little sea snail,
Sitting on the rocks
And when people walk by,
I can see their socks.

I am a spider in my web,
My name is Lee,
Yesterday I was lucky,
Cos I ate a bumblebee.

Hello, hello,
Caterpillar,
Eat some more and you'd
Be a *fatterpillar!*

I am an owl,
My name is Paige,
I am an actor,
My place is stage.

I am a bee,
I make honey,
I am a clown,
I am funny.

Joe Lockley (8)
Tividale Hall Primary School

MY HIDDEN TREASURE

As I walk through the breeze,
To my favourite place,
I gaze in the clouds,
Wait a minute,
Something's been altered,
I have another stare just to check,
Wow, it's really happening,
I see clouds fluffy like candyfloss,
I can almost feel it happening,
I reach out my hand, I can't reach,
I mustn't touch,
Am I the only one, who knows?
They are floating,
Animals are actually flying,
Pigs, giraffes and elephants,
I'm going with them,
Then I wake up,
It was a dream,
I stroke my hand through my hair,
I found my cloud; I'm keeping this as my hidden treasure.

Amrita Bisla (11)
Woodfield Junior School

HIDDEN TREASURES

I stepped inside,
I peered behind,
I felt my way onto the wall,
With my mighty claw.

I felt a breeze,
Touch my knees,
My hand slipped,
Then I tripped.

Suddenly a glowing gleam,
Appeared to my extreme,
A beam of light,
Shone so bright,
Then a big treasure chest rose,
I leapt back and struck a pose,
This was my secret.

Rohini Devi (10)
Woodfield Junior School

HIDDEN TREASURES
(My rat was (and still is) my treasure)

My rat used to lie on her hay,
Occasionally eating some rat food,
Awake each night and asleep each day,
Relaxing in a happy mood.

My rat used to play with her sister,
But then, one day, her sister died.
My rat really, really missed her,
If I had been her, I would've cried.

My rat became massive as she grew,
But something sadly went wrong.
Squelchy had a lump, actually two,
The vet said she wouldn't live for long.

I didn't really think about it much,
It didn't really sink in.
Squelchy gave the lump a little touch,
The lump was massive, under her chin.

But then, on the 16th Jan,
Three days before my birthday,
Squelchy's lump, under her chin,
Burst.

The vet had to put her down,
I couldn't help but cry,
I didn't really take it in,
That my rat was going to die.

I really loved my rat,
She was my *treasure.*

Cadi Evans (11)
Woodfield Junior School

HEAR, SEE, HOLD

Closer and closer,
Nearer and nearer,
Open the door,
I can hear her,
Softly crying,
My new baby sister.

Closer and closer,
Nearer and nearer,
Open the door,
I can see her,
Small, but chubby,
My new baby sister.

Closer and closer,
Nearer and nearer,
Open the door,
I can hold her,
Smiling up at me,
My new baby sister.

Lily Gelder (11)
Woodfield Junior School

HIDDEN STAR

You, star up there, gleaming so brightly,
Amongst your friends, compacted so tightly,
A jewel encrusted in a black, velvet cape,
Covering and darkening the wide landscape.
Not a whisper from you is heard,
Not a word, oh not a word.
So far away from me you are,
Oh gleaming, glistening, shining star.
Underneath I watch and stare,
Oh star, oh star, oh star up there.

Zoe Hunter-Grewal (11)
Woodfield Junior School

THE LAST LEAF FALLS

Floating, gliding, sailing onward,
Sailing, gliding, floating forward.
Not a whisper, not a sound,
Slowly drifting to the ground.

Veins are bold and stand out clear,
But no blood will pass through here.
Growing older, getting dry,
Getting blown around up high.

Seeing you, crinkled and dry,
Drifting slowly, passing by.
Nearing the dark and damp underneath,
Dying slowly,
The leaf.

Rosie Inman (11)
Woodfield Junior School

MY BROTHER'S SECRET BOX

My brother has a secret box
He is sick with chicken pox
I have to know what's in the box
I crept over floorboards like a sneaky fox

I opened the red, shiny door
But saw a big paw
There stood a big, pink poodle
That luckily was eating a noodle

There was the key upon the stool
The dog looked at me and started to drool
I picked up the key ever so quick
I'll be in the room in a tick

I opened the door
And there was a snore
The box was before me
I opened it so quietly
I couldn't believe my eyes
It was full to the brim
With air so thin.

Dan Jones (10)
Woodfield Junior School

I REMEMBER

I open a chest,
Full of water,
Full of shining glistening water,
Sparkling at its best.

I touch the cold, wet surface,
As it ripples and flows,
I fall right in
And swim around.

I'm not suffocating,
That's amazing,
I explore this watery world
And remember,
Remember water is something that must flow.

I look down into the deep
And see my most treasured memories
Forming in my head,
I'm home on dry land,
Thoughts must flow too,
I remember . . .

Nidhi Mehan (10)
Woodfield Junior School

SAUSAGES

When I am tired,
When I am glum,
When I've run out
Of bubblegum.
I'll shout it out,
Loud and clear,
'The sausages are here!'

They're big and juicy,
Round an' fat,
I treasure them,
More than my cat.
No one knows
How much I love them!
Sausages!
Sausages!
Sausages!

Claire Nellany (10)
Woodfield Junior School

THE CHEST

Twinkling brightly,
Shining like the stars at night,
Gems, jewels, gold, silver,
Piled in a great treasure chest,
Small like sand, great like boulders.

Daniel Owen (11)
Woodfield Junior School

THE DRAGON'S LAIR

Always take care,
When entering his lair,
Where the dragon lives.

There may be glittering gold,
But don't be too bold,
Where the dragon lives.

The dragon waited with fiery breath,
In came the knight and stabbed it to death,
It happened where the dragon lives.

Luke Price (10)
Woodfield Junior School

THE TREASURE CHEST

I was swimming in the sea
I got shoved by a wave
I opened my eyes
I was in a cave!

I saw a treasure chest
It was very, very old
I opened the lid
There was tons of gold!

I searched through the chest
I heard a little ping
There was a small glass jar
That held a diamond ring!

I took out the ring
I put it on
The cave started to shake
I was gone!

Naveed Raza (11)
Woodfield Junior School

THE PLATINUM BEAR STONE

Only the bravest will dare,
To face the ferocious bear,
For the valuable platinum bear stone.

Everyone is eaten whole,
Who tries to get through the hole,
To eliminate the bear for the stone.

A man slashed at the bear hard,
The man was severely scarred
And retrieved the valuable stone gladly.

James Robbins (10)
Woodfield Junior School

MY HIDDEN TREASURE

I have a treasure,
A big secret of mine
And this is why I'm writing this rhyme,
You will never see my hidden treasure,
Because it is my favourite pleasure.

It is not silver and it is not gold,
You will have to wait to behold,
I cannot wait
Before my fate.

My secret is inside me,
You'll have to wait and see,
My treasure is in front of your eyes.

My secret is the best thing in the world,
Love for my family is my hidden treasure,
Which you can never measure,
Love is my hidden treasure!

Jennifer Robbins (11)
Woodfield Junior School

HIDDEN TREASURES

Deep, deep down in the ocean of Bong,
Where the sand blows quickly around.
Something lies there beside the weeds,
Buried deeply in the sandy ground.

Tied on top of this big thing,
Was something that shone brightly.
It was a key that was not rusty,
Not even very slightly.

A diver tried to open the box,
The lid lifted a tiny bit
And then something glowed,
As though the box inside was lit.

She opened it fully to reveal the gold
And jewels and silver and bronze and more gold.
She gave a smile from ear to ear,
For this was a story to be told.

Maninder Saggu (11)
Woodfield Junior School

HIDDEN TREASURES

In a cave a dragon lay fast asleep
But over him treasures lay
I tiptoed carefully along the floor
There was no space
I had no choice
But to tiptoe carefully over
I got to the end
I sat down for a rest
'What's that lit up over there?' I said
It's a chest
I stuffed my pockets with coins and jewels
Then I felt a burn
It was the dragon!
I ran like mad and got out of the cave
Then I noticed
Everything fell out of my pockets except for one coin
I'm going to keep that as my hidden treasure.

Sodhi Sahota (10)
Woodfield Junior School

THE SECRET GARDEN

I woke up in the morning
I saw a flashing light,
I went up to the window
And it was flashing bright,
On the window sill,
There was a great big key,
There was a label stuck to it,
Which said it was for me,
I quickly put my glasses on
And saw a golden door,
I ran up very close to it
And slid the key inside,
It opened very smoothly
And I threw the key aside,
When I walked through the passage,
I looked at an amazing garden,
Where fruits where growing everywhere,
But then I woke up from my dream
And wished that I was there.

Adam Tustin (11)
Woodfield Junior School

PRIVACY

All alone in your home,
No one there at you to stare.

No one walking, no one talking,
No one dancing, no one prancing.

All alone in your home,
No one there at you to stare.

No one lying, no one crying,
No one taking, no one waking.

All alone in your home,
No one there at you to stare.

No one heaving, only breathing,
At its leisure, a hidden treasure.

All alone in your home,
No one there at you to stare.

Alec White (10)
Woodfield Junior School

THE HIDDEN HEART

Clink! Clonk!
A knight trudges through the mud,
Plink! Plonk!
Rain crashes down on his bloodstained armour,
Back from the battle, the only survivor.

His body is cold,
He has no heart,
A bloodstained murderer,
Wading through the mud and blood.

He finds his way home
And waiting for him is his child,
His body fills with warmth,
He's found his hidden treasure,
His heart.

Jonathan Woodall (10)
Woodfield Junior School

MY SECRET PLACE

My secret place is at the bottom of the garden,
It's certainly never a bore,
With two flowerpots and a jug at the window
And a homely *welcome* sign at the door.

My secret place is at the bottom of the garden,
It is comforting, I suppose, in a way,
The patched-up roof is damp and soggy,
With wet grass and hay!

My secret place is full of memories,
At every window and door,
Each one has a heart-warming memory
And when each year passes by, they grow even more!

Charlotte Kertrestel (11)
Wyken Croft Primary School

THE HUNT FOR HIDDEN TREASURE

Ahoy there shipmates
It's time to find some treasure
We'll have to go through pain
To get our golden pleasure

We'll have to dig all night
We'll have to dig all day
We'll have to dig 24 hours
According to what I say

We'll dig upon the sand
We'll dig deep under the sea
And when we find the treasure
There'll be enough for you and me!

We'll be rich with golden coins
We'll be as rich as ever can be
But really don't forget
We need the golden key!

Darren Haley (11)
Wyken Croft Primary School

HIDDEN TREASURES

What a pleasure to find hidden treasure:
In a grotto or a cave:
Or under the sea, way down deep,
Where an octopus might sleep.

Fish dart in and round about
And treasure hunters yell and shout.

Rubies - pearls and gold galore,
If we keep looking we may find more.

Leah Thompson (8)
Wyken Croft Primary School

HIDDEN TREASURES

H   elp me find the hidden treasure
I   'd like it if you could
D   iamonds, pearls and rubies lie in the chest
D   olphins swim around it
E   lectric eels dance beside it
N   ever, ever stop looking for the hidden treasures

T   onight we will prepare to find the treasure
R   eading the map as we go
E   ventually we will find it
A   rguments will begin for who's to keep the treasure
S   andy beaches will be covered with treasure
U   s and you will get to keep it
R   un quickly to the treasure
E   ventually you won't find it
S   o, go away because I have the *hidden treasure!*

Hope Roberts-Dalton (10)
Wyken Croft Primary School

HIDDEN TREASURE

Where may the treasure be?
It might be in the sea,
It could be on the land,
It could be in the sand.

Is it under a shell?
It could be in a ship's bell,
It could be in a toy,
No, it is inside a buoy.

David Sanders (10)
Wyken Croft Primary School